While I Wait

*Learning To Wait On
An Unanswered Promise*

Carolyn J Blue

While I Wait

Published by: LifeSkill® Institute, Inc.
Copyright © 2018 by Carolyn J. Blue

All rights reserved. No part of this book may be used, reproduced or transmitted in any form or by any means, electronic or mechanical, including photocopying and recording, or by any information storage or retrieval system, without written permission from the publisher, except by a reviewer who wishes to quote brief excerpts in connection with a group study, a review in a newspaper, magazine, or electronic publication.

Requests for permission should be addressed in writing to: Embracing It Now, Inc., P.O. Box 661 Leland, NC 28451

Library of Congress Cataloging-in-Publication Data

Blue, Carolyn J. 1963—
   While I Wait (Learning To Wait On An Unanswered Promise) by Carolyn J. Blue

   ISBN 978-1-890-199-03-6 paperback edition
   ISBN 978-1-890-199-04-3 hardcover edition

Library of Congress Control Number: 2018944200
   1. Religion   I. Title   II. Blue, Carolyn J.
   2. Self-Help/Self-Improvement
   3. Christian Life
   4. Women's Issues
   5. Spiritual Growth

Printed in the United States of America

Publisher:
Lifeskill Institute Inc. SAN: 255-8440
P.O. Box 302
Wilmington, NC 28402
(800) 570-4009

Email: info@embracingitnow.com
Website: www.embracingitnow.com

ACKNOWLEDGMENTS

First I am thankful to God for the inspiration to write this book, and for trusting me to share my experiences with the world. He could have chosen anyone else, but He chose me, and I'm grateful.

I am very grateful to my husband Eric, and my children Johnathan and Veronda for allowing me to share their stories, and for supporting me on this journey.

To my oldest daughter LaTanya Blue Rickman I'm so thankful for our everyday talks and for listening to me and encouraging me along the way, and reminding me that I could do it, and for constantly telling me how proud she is of me.

I am forever grateful to my daddy (Papa Joe) for instilling the desire to write my thoughts on paper, and for helping me with the prophetic messages through interpretation.

Tanya Millhouse I appreciate your love and support on this journey, and for helping me with the prophetic messages through interpretation.

To the world's best pastors and church family Apostles Ricky & Sandra Randolph and Uplifting Faith Ministries, Inc. for your prayers, love, and encouragement to fulfill my destiny, and to complete my assignment.

I can not say enough about my siblings Virginia, Tony, Josephine, Alfredia, Charles, Aldrina, Katrina, and Kwanisha for being there with me all the way. I love you guys.

Special thanks to my former student and editor Lakeshia Gause owner of K Content Solutions for pushing me to meet my deadlines, and for your love and support.

Acknowledgments

Words can not express my gratitude for my mentors Dr. Herbert Harris & Sandra Spaulding Hughes for your encouragement and support during this journey. Thanks for publishing my book.

I am so thankful to Carol Debnam (Mom) for all the prayers, love, and support over the years. It has been such a blessing!

I am extremely grateful to my lifelong friends and prayer partners Rhonda Watts, Samantha Smith, Sequoia Debnam, Shelia Marie Davis, Stephanie Knowlin, Tamika Bierlein, and Theo Mills who have prayed for me before and during this project.

And to the thousands of other people I did not name that encouraged me along this journey to keep pressing, and to not give up, THANK YOU!!!

Dedicated
To
Mary S. Jenkins

My Mama
&
My Best Friend

February 17, 1941 – March 9, 2014

Contents

INTRODUCTION	7
CHAPTER 1	9
My Wait Was Necessary	
CHAPTER 2	23
There's Purpose In Waiting	
CHAPTER 3	31
The Benefits Of Waiting	
CHAPTER 4	41
What Does It Mean To Wait	
CHAPTER 5	49
What Are You Waiting For?	
CHAPTER 6	61
The Importance Of Waiting	
CHAPTER 7	69
Learn How To Wait	
CHAPTER 8	77
Because I Waited	
CHAPTER 9	85
Waiting Pitfalls	
CHAPTER 10	93
How Do You Wait?	
CONCLUSION	101
ABOUT THE AUTHOR	103

Introduction

I imagine myself standing on the outside of a bubble looking in, and in this bubble, is everything that I have experienced up to this point in my life. I see the good, the bad, and the ugly. I see my ups and my downs, and say to myself, "If only I knew then what I know now, I would not have gone through half of the situations and storms I have been through." The reflection of my life in the bubble helped me realize that there were times in my life where I could have avoided some of my delays, but because of my disobedience and selfishness my process was longer. My view in the bubble prompted my desire to help others avoid the downward spiral of delays that I experienced in my life while waiting on an unanswered promise.

The purpose for me writing this book, is to answer the question "What do I want my readers to know about waiting"? My desire is, as you read this book, and find yourself in the midst of, or better yet, at the beginning of your situations like the "old me in the bubble," you will learn from my life lessons. I am sure you too have said, "If I knew this then, I would not have gone through as many unnecessary steps." This book is relatively short, but to the point, and will teach you a depth of truth. As you read the words on each page, allow them to penetrate your heart, and move you to apply every truth to your life. I chose to be transparent about my journey because I learned the hard way what it means to wait.

Learning the truths in this book will save you some heartaches and disappointments I experienced while learning what to do while you wait for the manifestation of your promises and blessings. My prayer is that you will escape what I have gone through and that during your waiting process, you will:

Gain an understanding of why you wait,
Learn the definition of waiting,
Know the meaning of what you are waiting for,
Be able to accomplish your goals,
Complete your assigned purpose without having to waste unnecessary time and energy,
Achieve and walk entirely in the purpose for which God has created you.

My hope is that you will see a reflection of yourself while reading this book and rely on God for instructions in your season of waiting. Understand that this is not just another book or just something to do, but that: You will truly be blessed if you are willing to open up your heart and your spirit to receive what God is saying as He speaks to me, and as I speak to you through the pages of this book. You will not only be blessed, but you will be delivered and freed from those issues and situations that are hindering you while you find solutions to what it means to wait, and what to do while you wait. You will experience freedom from anything that is hindering you from getting where you need to be at the end of your waiting period.

During this waiting period, let me reassure you that you are not standing still because you can not see the answers that God has given you, knowing that you should have moved into your victory.

As you read this book, allow God to minister to you, see yourself in each scenario, be transparent, and know that God will elevate you through your season of waiting. In your next level of elevation, may you be blessed, highly favored, and set free in the words that are spoken on these pages. Then I will know that God has accomplished what He needed to do in my life, and in my season of waiting.

My Wait Was Necessary - The Causes and Effects of Waiting

Chapter 1

On November 8, 2000, I faced a traumatic situation that changed my life. I was eight months pregnant with our youngest child (Veronda), and had just moved into our new dream home one month prior. I was out of work due to complications with my pregnancy, our ten-year-old son (Johnathan) was in private school, and my husband (Eric) who spent the last twenty-eight and a half years with one company, came home and broke the news that he was fired from his job. Our insurance coverage was gone in a flash, our son's tuition was due, and we were facing a brand new mortgage to only name a few things. Talk about a significant shift not only in our lifestyle, but our lives. Our lives were tilted out of balance to the fullest degree.

This life altering experience taught me the importance of trusting God when life is good, and when your world is out of alignment. After a huge sigh, I told my husband that God knows and He cares, and that everything would be fine, and would work out for our good. All of those words I was uttering to him sounded good, but I could sense from his demeanor that he was listening to me, but thinking "I hear what you're saying, I know what you're saying, I want to believe what you are saying, but there is a part of me that still feels afraid." He was trying to remain strong for me, and I was attempting to maintain emotional balance for him, but the bottom line was that we witnessed firsthand that life can change dramatically in a matter of minutes.

Where do we go from here? How will we manage our financial obligations? How will we care for our family?

What did we do wrong? How could this happen to us? How will we ever find balance? All of these questions crowded my mind as I reflected on our life as I knew it. A life where we were financially stable enough to support everyone else in time of need, travel wherever we wanted to go, purchase what we wanted, help others when they were in need, and be a blessing to those we came in contact with, was now changed right before our eyes.

What steps do you take when you are faced with a crisis, and about to lose everything that you have ever owned? Where do you turn when you have tried and tried, you have exhausted your resources, yet it seems like all hell is breaking loose in your life from every angle? I didn't know which way to turn, or how to find balance, but I knew that I were facing a "9-1-1 emergency." I cried out to the Lord, reminding Him of His word, and His promises. I remember telling Him that I knew He was the God of Abraham, Isaac, and Jacob, and I also knew He was my God, and I could not do this on my own, so I needed Him to teach me what to do while I wait.

Our "American Dream" was delayed for a season, and I found myself questioning God about why He allowed this heartache to happen to me. My world was turned upside down, and my life was totally out of balance. The loss of a job, a new home, a new baby, and a multitude of unpaid bills enhanced the relationship issues in our marriage. My husband who was accustomed to taking care of his family, and providing everything for us "in the natural" began to shut down and stopped communicating with me, which changed the direction of our relationship. At the time, I was a certified relationship coach spending multiple hours counseling other couples week after week, but could not prevent my marriage from unraveling at the seams. This catastrophe compounded everything else that I had going on at the time and pushed me back for a moment, leaving me unsure of how to realign my life and move forward.

Prior to our life altering situation, I received multiple prophetic messages that stated, I was going to be very successful and prosperous, that everything my hands touched would prosper, and every place my feet would tread, I would possess the territory. All of the prophecies were relevant to the journey I was on. I believed them, pondered them in my heart, even experienced some of them, but all of a sudden it appeared that my dreams were shattered. In the midst of my chaos, and dismay, I remember hearing the voice of the Lord say "I am your provider, I am Jehovah Jireh. I am the God who provides, everything else is a resource, but I am your true source. Those words shifted my mindset, and prompted me to look past my current situation. I had a decision to make: to completely trust God or to allow my problems to overtake me. I felt my problems drowning me in misery, and I began to sink. I had a pity party, and my emotions were all over the place, but it did not take long to come to myself like the prodigal son (Luke 15).

> *11 To illustrate the point further, Jesus told them this story: "A man had two sons. 12 The younger son told his father, 'I want my share of your estate now before you die.' So his father agreed to divide his wealth between his sons.*
> *13 "A few days later this younger son packed all his belongings and moved to a distant land, and there he wasted all his money in wild living. 14 About the time his money ran out, a great famine swept over the land, and he began to starve. 15 He persuaded a local farmer to hire him, and the man sent him into*

his fields to feed the pigs. **16** The young man became so hungry that even the pods he was feeding the pigs looked good to him. But no one gave him anything.

17 "When he finally came to his senses, he said to himself, 'At home even the hired servants have food enough to spare, and here I am dying of hunger! **18** I will go home to my father and say, "Father, I have sinned against both heaven and you,**19** and I am no longer worthy of being called your son. Please take me on as a hired servant."'

20 "So he returned home to his father. And while he was still a long way off, his father saw him coming. Filled with love and compassion, he ran to his son, embraced him, and kissed him. **21** His son said to him, 'Father, I have sinned against both heaven and you, and I am no longer worthy of being called your son.[a]'

22 "But his father said to the servants, 'Quick! Bring the finest robe in the house and put it on him. Get a ring for his finger and sandals for his feet. **23** And kill the calf we have been fattening. We must celebrate with a feast, **24** for this son of mine was dead and has now returned to life. He was lost, but now he is found.' So the party began.

25 "Meanwhile, the older son was in the fields working. When he returned home, he heard music and dancing in the house, **26** and he asked one of the servants what was going on. **27** 'Your brother is back,' he was told, 'and your father has killed the fat-

> *tened calf. We are celebrating because of his safe return.'*
> **28** *"The older brother was angry and wouldn't go in. His father came out and begged him,* **29** *but he replied, 'All these years I've slaved for you and never once refused to do a single thing you told me to. And in all that time you never gave me even one young goat for a feast with my friends.* **30** *Yet when this son of yours comes back after squandering your money on prostitutes, you celebrate by killing the fattened calf!'*
> **31** *"His father said to him, 'Look, dear son, you have always stayed by me, and everything I have is yours.* **32** *We had to celebrate this happy day. For your brother was dead and has come back to life! He was lost, but now he is found!*

I came to myself and made a decision that I would seek balance and press forward while I wait. You too, have encountered different types of life-altering events that have pushed you backward, suppressed your dreams, and may have even caused a delay in obtaining your heart's desires. But on this day, I decree and declare unto you that when you choose to wait on Him, every promise in His book, every word that He spoke in your life, every heart's desire you have, shall be yours, when you take delight in the Lord, and He will give you your heart's desires. (Psalm 37: 4).

> **4** *Take delight in the Lord, and he will give you your heart's desires.*

This challenging experience forced me to wait on Him, and I mean literally because I didn't have a choice. Going through this life-altering encounter, resulted in my husband experiencing depression and anxiety, which led to him shutting out the world. Of course, this included me, and at that time, I became his worst enemy. In the midst of going through all of our turmoil and chaos, my greatest desire was to save our marriage. All I wanted was for him to love me the way he had in the past, and to be there to protect me and our children. For the most part, I trusted God to take care of everything else, but during this process, I failed drastically with the scripture that says trust in the Lord with ALL of my heart and lean not to my understanding, in ALL my ways acknowledge Him (Proverbs 3:5-6).

> *5* Trust in the Lord with all thine heart; and lean not unto thine own understanding. *6* In all thy ways acknowledge him, and he shall direct thy paths.

I missed the word **ALL**. I trusted God to handle every area of my life, except my marriage.

Many men like my husband, tend to equate their success with their jobs. When their jobs are in tact, they usually say everything is great, no matter what may be going on. As a result of losing his job, he was stuck in his past, and struggled to move past his perceived emotions of unfair treatment. Over a period of time, he worked a few odd jobs, but nothing worked out because his life was out of balance due to him experiencing significant depression. If I suggested, "It is nice weather outside today, let's go do something together," he would say "No it looks cloudy outside, and I don't feel like doing anything today." If I said "We don't have to go out tonight let's just plan a quiet dinner here at the house and watch a movie," he would say something along the lines of "You know we can't afford to buy anything extra, and

I don't feel much like doing anything." Long story short, as a result of the traumatic experience he encountered from losing his job, every area of our relationship was tested. I was forced to learn what to do while I wait for the storm to pass.

Have you ever been in a situation where you know what God has promised, you believe what he has promised, you are standing on that promise, but everything is going crazy all around you? You have waited and waited, but your life is still the same or even worse. That was my life, but despite what the devil made it look like, despite how the devil made me feel, despite what the devil made it appear to be, I had to decide whether or not to stand on God's word. I was at a crossroad about moving forward in my crisis and even though I believed He was going to bring me through it, the question was, could I trust Him enough to handle it while I wait during this challenging time? The more I attempted to make our marriage work and spend time communicating with my husband, the more he pulled away. Our relationship became strained, and the more challenging it became, the more I realized I did not have a choice but to trust God while I wait.

One summer, my family planned a mini vacation, but because I was so desperate to save my marriage, I sent our children, and stayed behind in an effort to work things out. You guessed it! It was a very long weekend! My family returned home only to discover that my weekend was a disaster. I kept attempting to make things right, by trying to fix the marriage. I was trying to make him happy, and I tried to ease the pain. But then I realized, it was all **ME** trying to make the marriage work.

Before Eric lost his job, he worked all the time, and in my mind, he was a workaholic. He loved what he did, and was loyal to the company, but the problem for me was that he was gone all the time. By the time he would get home, it would be time to eat dinner, and get rest for the next day. This eventually led to me experiencing insecurities, and loneliness. I knew he was doing it for our family, and he was trying to make the best life for us, but his excessive work schedule caused a significant disruption in our relationship. His frequent absence from home, left me with too much alone time to think.

Reflecting on it when looking in the bubble, I should have been somewhere praying and asking God to cover and protect my man while he was out working. However, instead of me turning to God, I sat at home having a pity party about him not being home with us or at some function that I can't even remember now. Over time I began to question his love for me, and if it had changed. This may sound crazy to some, but it was my reality. I know that there are some of you that can relate to my drama. Your spouse is a hard-working individual, but over a period, the communication has spiraled downward, and intimacy in the marriage has dwindled down. This type of disruption in your relationship can pose a significant problem in your marriage if you lose focus on what is essential.

I was focused on all the wrong things for years, and I remember telling him that I hated his job, because he was always at work, and never had time for me. We all have some unanswered questions about our mate when we are in a relationship, but when we have a godly spouse, it is good practice to Stop, Drop, and Cover, (**Stop** whining and complaining, **Drop** everything, and **Cover** your mate in prayer). This was a major problem in my relationship that went unaddressed for years and made my time of waiting necessary.

Another reason my wait was necessary was because I was living in a fantasy world. I expected everything to be perfect in our relationship. He spoiled me when we first met and started to build our relationship. We could not get enough of spending time with each other, even though he worked all the time when we first met. Over a period, we both became complacent in our marriage and stopped dating each other. He was focused on our dreams and goals and wanted things to come to pass for us. He worked hard to accomplish our dreams so that we could play later, but I became selfish and self-righteous. I was only thinking about me and forgot about the fact that it was a family effort.

Eventually, I got tired of waiting for our marriage to be restored, and grew weary in my well-doing. I began to walk in fear that my marriage was falling apart and released fear in the atmosphere. I thought about us breaking up all the time. Therefore, what I feared most came to past. My marriage suffered and ended in divorce because I chose fear over faith while I was waiting on God.

Prophetic Message

One of the hardest things for human beings to do in the flesh is this thing called waiting. Even those that do not have a relationship with God understand the importance of patience and waiting. Every area in your life calls for you to wait on an everyday basis. You wait at the stop sign, you wait on the seasons, and there are some areas of waiting that are out of your control. It is in those areas that people get impatient and try to move forward on their own. Sarah provided a great example of getting restless and trying to move forward on her own without waiting on God (Genesis 16).

> *1 Now Sarai, Abram's wife, had not been able to bear children for him. But she had an Egyptian servant named Hagar. 2 So Sarai said to Abram, "The Lord has prevented me from having children. Go and sleep with my servant. Perhaps I can have children through her." And Abram agreed with Sarai's proposal. 3 So Sarai, Abram's wife, took Hagar the Egyptian servant and gave her to Abram as a wife. (This happened ten years after Abram had settled in the land of Canaan.)*
> *4 So Abram had sexual relations with Hagar, and she became pregnant. But when Hagar knew she was pregnant, she began to treat her mistress, Sarai, with contempt. 5 Then Sarai said to Abram, "This is all your fault! I put my servant into your arms, but now that she's pregnant she treats me with contempt. The Lord will show who's wrong—you or me!" 6 Abram replied, "Look, she is your servant, so deal with her*

as you see fit." Then Sarai treated Hagar so harshly that she finally ran away. **7** *The angel of the Lord found Hagar beside a spring of water in the wilderness, along the road to Shur.* **8** *The angel said to her, "Hagar, Sarai's servant, where have you come from, and where are you going?" "I'm running away from my mistress, Sarai," she replied.* **9** *The angel of the Lord said to her, "Return to your mistress, and submit to her authority."* **10** *Then he added, "I will give you more descendants than you can count."* **11** *And the angel also said, "You are now pregnant and will give birth to a son. You are to name him Ishmael (which means 'God hears'), for the Lord has heard your cry of distress.* **12** *This son of yours will be a wild man, as untamed as a wild donkey! He will raise his fist against everyone, and everyone will be against him. Yes, he will live in open hostility against all his relatives."* **13** *Thereafter, Hagar used another name to refer to the Lord, who had spoken to her. She said, "You are the God who sees me." She also said, "Have I truly seen the One who sees me?"* **14** *So that well was named Beer-lahai-roi (which means "well of the Living One who sees me"). It can still be found between Kadesh and Bered.* **15** *So Hagar gave Abram a son, and Abram named him Ishmael.* **16** *Abram was eighty-six years old when Ishmael was born.*

The path that you travel sometimes changes the very course that you are set on, but it is important to wait on a daily basis, weekly basis, monthly basis, and even on an annual basis. No one can define the waiting period except God. Nobody can understand the reason for waiting except God. It is essential to understand the causes and effects of waiting: you will suffer consequences of not waiting, yet you will reap benefits for waiting. Remember waiting is necessary, but it is a choice that you must make:

> (a) If you wait, you will reap the benefits of waiting,
> (b) If you do not wait, you will suffer the consequences of not waiting.

These are the causes and effects of waiting.

My Wait Was Necessary - The Causes and Effects of Waiting

Chapter 1 — Notes

My Wait Was Necessary **While I Wait**

There's Purpose In Waiting

Chapter 2

Just as the wait was necessary for me, I believe that there is also purpose in your waiting as well. You should wait with expectation to receive every blessing that God has promised you, and every blessing you have been asking of Him. Whatever you asked Him for, and whatever he has promised to fulfill, I say unto you today, it will be worth the wait. If you are waiting for a restored relationship, a family, a job, healing, a deliverance, a breakthrough, or to take on the mind of Christ, there's purpose in waiting.

God is a promise keeper, and when we trust and believe Him, He is a rewarder of those who diligently seek after Him (Hebrews 11:6).

> *6 But without faith it is impossible to please him: for he that cometh to God must believe that he is, and that he is a rewarder of them that diligently seek him.*

It doesn't matter what things look like, nor does it matter how chaotic your life has become. If you stay focused and keep pushing forward, your blessings will come to pass. Focus on the results of waiting, rather than the process of waiting.

It is also important to wait because it stretches and strengthens you, and adds strength to your muscles. It reinforces your spiritual muscles, as well as your emotional and physical muscles. We must learn endurance while we wait because waiting is not always comfortable. Are you ready to receive what God has for you? Are you ready for the portal of heaven to open and pour out your blessings? If so, you must be willing to wait while you are going through your difficult seasons. Do not get in a hurry as I did, and miss your blessing. You must be willing to wait while going through your trials and situations at all costs. Remember to whom much is given much is required (Luke 12:48).

> **48** *But someone who does not know, and then does something wrong, will be punished only lightly. When someone has been given much, much will be required in return; and when someone has been entrusted with much, even more will be required.*

You cannot expect to receive the blessings you have been waiting for, and not experience any friction. While you wait, you must be willing to endure as a good soldier. You should not murmur and complain when things are not going the way you expect them to go, but you must trust the God of Abraham, Isaac, and Jacob to see you through to your expected end.

When I was going through turmoil in my marriage, I waited on God initially, but it was not long before I became impatient and started taking matters into my own hands. I tried to rush God, and bargain with Him to fix things. I attempted to help Him out because, in my desperation, I believed it was taking Him too long to answer my prayers. My marriage meant the whole world to me, and I lost focus of everything else during that time. I was so focused on the fact that I wanted a "right now" restoration, in my marriage, and with my husband's job situation. I wanted to see things turned around right then, and I did not want to wait any longer. I was struggling with the aspect of what God was pushing me to pursue, which was "to trust." I eventually got ahead of God and missed His timing concerning my marriage. I realized it was a process that he was taking me through, but not the fact that I needed to trust Him entirely. The only details I could focus on were how I felt rejected, frustrated, angry, and unworthy. I thought about how I minister to so many others, and help them in their relationships and situations, but could do nothing to stop my marriage from crumbling.

I was not patient at the time and was not interested in listening to anything God had to say. My negative attitude caused a delay in the release of my blessings. I missed the instructions He was trying to give me because I was not listening.

God is a specific God! He had a particular process He wanted to take me through to release my blessings, and He wants to do the same thing for you. You must be in tune with His voice to receive His message and His grace. It is critical to seek God for the necessary steps of waiting, and then follow those steps as He gives them. We trust the Lord and acknowledge Him in everything we do and not lean to our own understanding and allow Him to direct our path (Proverbs 3:6).

6 Seek his will in all you do, and he will show you which path to take.

This scripture is not just for this situation, but is necessary for every aspect of your life. Let's talk about the purpose in the waiting in order to receive the manifestation of that which you are expecting. Whatever God has promised you, He's going to do it. We must hold fast to the promise because He will fulfill every promise, even if it is at the eleventh hour. We must wait on Him. When you decide to wait, just know that there are benefits to waiting. There is such a blessing in waiting. When you wait, you will experience His divine promise. In His divine promise everything that you desire when you delight yourself in Him, He will give you the desires of your heart (Psalm 37:4).

> *4 Delight thyself also in the LORD; and he shall give thee the desires of thine heart.*

Therefore, because you delight yourself in Him, you are eligible for the divine promise.

My wait was also necessary because while I was preaching and teaching the word of God and helping everybody else, I failed to minister to my own husband's needs. I took care of everyone except him. I literally made another life for myself just to escape our issues, and how I was really feeling on the inside. Everybody on the outside thought we had a perfect marriage, but little did they know. This fact alone proves it is not good to share your business with everybody, but it is okay to find someone you can seek godly counsel from or somebody who has experienced what you are going through. They should give you suggestions on how to improve your relationship.

During my time of waiting, I continued to minister, I continued to teach, study, and pray, but I did not receive the words in my heart. After all of that, at the end of each day, I still found myself alone and lonely, frustrated and disgusted. Why? Because I believed the promises God had spoken to me concerning my marriage, concerning my life and dreams were shattered right before my eyes. As a result of my failing marriage, I began spending time listening to the wrong voices rather than the voice of God. When people would call, I spent my time listening to them and began allowing their negativity to get the best of me. I knew things were not quite right when I started listening to that negative stuff and allowed it to affect me and eventually resulted in me becoming numb to what was going on in my house.

Prophetic Message

There is a saying that people have heard many times that "should you continue doing the same thing the same way you get the same results." I believe man has defined this as insanity. So why not look at it spiritually. Would you consider it to be insanity to choose to not wait on God? Not the god of the world, but would you consider it to be insane not to wait on such a supernatural and awesome God! Why not wait on a God that has created the heavens and the earth? Why not wait on a God that can put a rainbow in the sky?

Why not wait on a God that also knows to tell the ocean how far to come? Why not wait on a God like that? Is that insanity? Yet in the small mind of man, I say in the small mind of man because man's mind is nowhere near the realm of the mind of God. So day in and day out, man continues to do the same thing over and over and getting the same results. At some point, you should think "If I just waited, then I would not have to go through this." Sometimes we get to the point that we say "If I do this, then I explain to myself that, yes this is the way that God wanted me to do it." We don't even ask Him or wait for instructions.

So yet at some point, He steps back and says "If you're gonna do it, then let Me take my hands off of it, and let you see. " Until you learn the lesson, you will continue to repeat the same things. So step aside and let God be the God that He is, the God of all things, the God of all mankind. He is the creator of all good and perfect gifts (James 1:17).

> *17 Every good gift and every perfect gift is from above, and cometh down from the Father of lights, with whom is no variableness, neither shadow of turning.*

Step aside and let Him be God in your life. If you continue to do things the same way, you will continue to get the same results. You will be even more frustrated, and you are going to continue to ask the same question "What am I waiting for?" So at some point in time, say yes, mean it, and step aside and let God do what He does and that is be God. He changeth not and He will be God (Malachi 3:6).

> *6 I am the LORD, and I do not change. That is why you descendants of Jacob are not already destroyed.*

Every day in His kingdom shall be a different day, if you just wait.

There's Purpose In Waiting

Chapter 2 — Notes

There's Purpose In Waiting　　　　　　　**While I Wait**

The Benefits Of Waiting

Chapter 3

A divine promise is a promise that was made by God to only be delivered through and by Him. It is a promise that man cannot give us. It is a promise that cannot be duplicated, no matter what man tries to do. It is a promise that to the natural eyes, there is no way you can receive it, except God Almighty uses His Sovereign ability to infiltrate things in the heaven to become a reality. The benefits of waiting results in awesome blessings.

I received my divine promise after I made a decision to wait on God, and went through the necessary process of waiting. On November 22, 2009, a close relative who helped us raise our children died unexpectedly. Her death changed the course of my life, knowing she was no longer here to impart in my children's life. In the midst of my pain, God used her death to birth life in our dead situation. My husband and I reconnected after having minimal contact during our three-year separation and divorce. Nobody but God brought us back together. Our reunion did not happen overnight nor because I was sitting around twiddling my fingers or talking on my phone or because he was sitting around doing nothing. We both had been seeking God for a change within us. Our desire to want more of God, to learn more about His desire for our lives, and to be more like him, brought about a change in the two of us. This hunger for Him and the change activated our divine promise.

During this time of waiting, we learned more about who God was, and what He really wanted for us. Learning to wait helped us overcome our selfishness, as we grew spiritually, and gained clarity of why our marriage suffered the first time. We both understood why we were in such a warfare during our marriage. We allowed the enemy access to our lives, and our issues, which literally destroyed our marriage.

When you are waiting on God to answer your prayers, and manifest His promises, it is important to keep your eyes on the blessings to avoid distractions that will consume your focus and cause you to miss your benefits. I was guilty of allowing distractions to overtake my thinking, and get in my spirit; which resulted in me lacking balance and losing focus of my blessing. This season of waiting taught me how to access my benefits. When distractions come, because they will come, you must know how to war in the spirit and know how to recognize them in order to send them back to the pits of hell in the beginning.

Another benefit of waiting is learning to be thankful in the midst of what you are going through. God has allowed you to go through this process, and He is clear on where He is taking you. The Bible says in all things give thanks (1Thessalonians 5:18).

18 Be thankful in all circumstances, for this is God's will for you who belong to Christ Jesus.

I love this scripture because in the midst of my storm, although I was very emotional, I had to get past my anger and feelings of rejection, and tell God thank you. I thanked Him that the situation was not as bad as it could have been nor as bad as some marriages I know of. When Eric and I separated, we were not angry with each other, we were angry with the situation that we allowed to destroy what God had put together. The bible says what God joined together; let no man put asunder (Mark 10:9).

9 let no one split apart what God has joined together.

The Benefits Of Waiting

We allowed the enemy to come in and shift our marriage, which caused us to experience a lack of balance. The good news is that when we took on the mind of Christ and took our minds off of ourselves, God restored all of our brokenness (Philippians 2:5).

5 Let this mind be in you, which was also in Christ Jesus.

When we wait on the Lord with thanksgiving, there is nothing that will be denied (1 Timothy 4:4).

4 For everything God created is good, and nothing is to be rejected if it is received with thanksgiving.

This is the ultimate benefit of waiting.

When we wait, that means we trust. When we wait, it means that we have faith. When we wait, it means we believe that God will do what He said He will do. Even if life is not going the way you expect it to go, you can't believe God one minute, and doubt Him the next. You must know that even if it does not look like it things are getting better, which allows us to keep believing and moving forward. When it looks like you are taking a step backward, do not lose hope. Hold fast to your faith, balance your steps, and balance your thinking so that you can receive the benefits by doing what God tells you to do.

Waiting is a choice like anything else. We can choose to wait or not, but there are benefits to waiting and consequences to not waiting. I would have missed what God had for me if I had not changed the way I was thinking or had I chosen to continue along the path of "Why did this happen to me or was God in this, or why did God allow this?" However, because of my willingness to humble myself, and balance my thinking, God heard my earnest cry, and honored my repentant heart as I prayed "God I'm sorry, and I repent for what I have said and done, and for what I have not done."

There is also a spiritual maturity in waiting because just as we mature age-wise we have to do the same thing spiritually. When you are mature, it takes the anxiousness out of waiting. When you go through the maturity process, you are refined and come through different then when you started. You will not be the same when you come through the waiting process. Would you want to come out the same? Believe it or not people do not look the same when they are going through a spiritual process.

We look at what the situation looks like right now, rather than seeing at what the situation will look like when God puts His hands on it. We get caught up in the now, and because we get so caught up in the now, we miss the "then". We can't see the "then" because we are stuck in the now. That is part of the distraction as well, because it is not great big things. Sometimes it is little things that take our attention away from that waiting process. We have to learn to not sweat the small stuff. After you've gone through the process then you can see it, but you can't see it in the middle of the process. It was necessary to grow me spiritually.

The entire marriage had to be renewed before God. I made up my mind that I needed to wait on God. I messed up and literally had to trust God in all of it. I became angry when it was over. I did it as a result of all the rejection and heartache. My attitude was that of "I am not doing this, I do not have to do this, I am better off by myself." Then whenever it was over, I became angry and upset. How could I minister to the world and tell them how awesome marriage is, coaching married couples, counseling families, and my marriage was torn apart. I remember the Lord speaking to me ,telling me that I had made a god out of my husband. He had become my god, and His question to me was "Is it worth it to release him in order to gain it all." God had to get my complete attention, and I told Him "Yes God, it is worth me losing him. He told me to trust Him." At that point I released it from my heart. I had released him physically, but he was still connected to my heart. Once I released him, that heartstring, and that soul tie, then God began a work within the two of us. What I did not know was at the same time I was believing God to do a work in me, and wanting God to change me, Eric was praying the same prayer. He was seeking God as well for God to change him. I did not know this, because there was no communication between us, and because I decided not to wait on God, I did not find out until after the fact.

Death brought us back together. Death brought forth life, and God allowed us to come back together. Our marriage is totally different, all because of the wait. I believe that forgiveness was an essential part of our process because I do not remember any negative aspects of our relationship. It was like the entire slate was wiped clean. When I tell you He wiped the whole slate clean, it was wiped away, everything! Every hurt, every disappointment, every harsh word, every bit of rejection, every sleepless night, and every teardrop was gone! That's how I know God did it with His Good Self! I know that it was a benefit because I waited. If He did it for me, whatever it is, if it is promised to you, His promises are yes, when you will wait (2 Corinthians 1:20)

> **20** *For all the promises of God in him are yea, and in him Amen, unto the glory of God by us.*

I do not care what it is, If He promised it, He will do it for you because He has no respect of person (Romans 2:11)

11 For there is no respect of persons with God.

Prophetic Message

The simplest way to understand the benefits of waiting is to think of a benefits package. It is just like anything in your life that comes with a benefits package. In the word, it defines what your benefits are and your relationship with God. It is a package that reaps a lot of benefits, which you otherwise would not be able to have. When you look at this benefits package, some of the options sound good to you, some of them maybe so-so, but it is still a part of the package. As a part of the benefits package, you have to complete the forms. These forms are in the natural, but there are things you have to complete in the spirit in order to activate the benefits package. The difference between the benefits package in the world and the benefits package in the spirit is that the benefit package in the spirit does not have a waiting period.

When you say yes and come into a relationship with God you must understand that your benefits are already activated. So it is up to you to take advantage of the benefits that He is offering to you, and you must understand the benefits that He is offering to you. That is why He sent His word. If you read His word, you will have a better understanding of the awesome benefits package that you have. You have life insurance, you have vision, you have dental, you have medical, and these benefits, do not even have a co-pay, because He's already paid for it. Jesus paid for them with His blood. They are bought at a high price. They were paid for with His blood that was shed over two thousand years ago. You don't have to worry about whether or not these benefits are going to expire. Just take advantage of the benefits when you say yes. Even though some of them may not be released to you in the very beginning, understand that as you walk through the process, as the doors are opened unto you, benefit after benefit is going to be released unto you!

He is not going to release them unto you until you are in that stage and in that period that you are ready to receive them. Oftentimes people think that they are ready to receive benefits, but God says to you, as the most High God, as your creator, that some of these benefits come with a price, and as you go through the refining process, that is when these benefits will be released unto you. You will be spiritually mature enough to receive the benefits and you will be spiritually mature enough to know how to use the benefit. You will use these benefits not only to your satisfaction but also to be a blessing to others that are not at the place where this same benefit has been released unto them. God says unto you, do not compare your benefits package with benefit packages of others, because they are individual benefits packages. They are based on your specific needs. These needs were defined even before you came into this world. They were defined supernaturally.

Everybody, when they came into this world, had a benefits package with their name written on it, and as you went through the process, the benefits were released unto you. If there is still a benefit that you are waiting on, according to God's word, as you are looking at others' benefit packages, don't compare yourself or your package to others. There is not an option when it comes to the benefit plans in the supernatural and in the spirit. You either choose the entire benefits package or none because it is a personalized package. It is an individual package. Because in the natural, when you have a benefits package, it is designed just for that group. But God says this is an individual package designed just for each and every one of us.

Your benefits package is based on your level of faith, it is based on where you are going, it is based on where you are. So ask yourself the question, this benefit that I am asking for, first of all, am I ready for it, do I want it for selfish gain, for selfish purposes, or do I want it in order to be able to be a blessing to others in the Body of Christ? Once you have answered this, then you will understand why that particular benefit has not been released unto you yet. Are your hands big enough to receive this benefit, are your eyes tuned enough to see the benefit, are your ears open enough to hear the benefit, and are you in a place that when you open your mouth and when you speak to release the benefit, because you have to remember that the power of life and death lies in your tongue, and that is a benefit.

Therefore, in that benefit, are you speaking life or are you speaking death? You have to examine the whole benefits package. You see this benefits package is not in pieces, it is for you to accept the whole part. You can't accept the medical without accepting the vision; you can't accept the dental without accepting the life. Once you accept the life, you accept the all the parts of the benefits package. So you have to ask yourself the question, am I really ready to receive of the benefits package, and if your answer is yes, then know that as you go on this journey that your benefits shall be released unto you by the Most High God.

The Benefits Of Waiting

Chapter 3 — Notes

What Does It Mean To Wait - Define Waiting

Chapter 4

Waiting, in general, can be difficult when you are accustomed to receiving things immediately. It can be very stressful if you are desperate for a change and you are forced to wait. To wait has several meanings that we will discuss. It means to hold on until, it means eagerly anticipating something is about to happen, and it means to serve others while you wait.

There are times you grow tired while waiting on God to answer your prayers or to come through on your behalf, and your situation seems insurmountable. You have prayed, you have fasted, and you have cried out to God, to no avail. You feel yourself losing your balance as life's circumstances continuously push you against the wall. I know that you do not see any light at the end of the tunnel, but if you can just grab hold to the truth that every storm comes to an end, your wait will be endurable. When you totally trust God to order your steps, anything you are going through will be bearable because He will give you a way of escape (Psalm 119:133 & 1 Corinthians 10:13)

> *133 Guide my steps by your word, so I will not be overcome by evil.*
>
> *13 The temptations in your life are no different from what others experience. And God is faithful. He will not allow the temptation to be more than you can stand.*

When you are tempted, he will show you a way out so that you can endure. Many times God will give us an immediate answer, but sometimes He desires us to wait. Learning to wait is taught through experience. Think about how children respond when they ask a parent for a toy, and the parent says wait. The children continue to ask for that toy despite the fact that the parent has not changed his/her mind. They may have a temper tantrum and cry because they do not want to wait, and have to be taught what it means to wait. As parents, we sometimes talk to the child about what it means to wait, but sometimes when the child acts out of character, we have to teach the lesson of waiting by forcing the child to wait longer than usual for the toy. This is the same concept for us pertaining to God. When we ask Him to bless us or to bring us out of our situation, when God says to wait or does not say anything, if we obey Him, the answer comes sooner. However, when we throw a temper tantrum, the wait takes much longer. Therefore, it is in our best interest to trust that God knows and He cares about what we are experiencing, and He will never leave us nor forsake us (Hebrews 13:5).

> *5 Keep your lives free from the love of money and be content with what you have, because God has said, "Never will I leave you; never will I forsake you."*

I remember learning what it meant to wait, the hard way because I was hard-headed. It was the day of my initial sermon, and my husband did not show up to support me because he was unchurched at the time due to church hurt. A prophet had warned me that he was going to experience a season where he would not be in church, but after a few trials, he would be back. Although I knew the end result would be his return to church, I wanted him to be there for my special day. I was hurt, angry, embarrassed, and disappointed that he let me down. I could have saved myself some heartache and suffering if only I had believed the word of God, but I did not want to wait. That particular experience taught me that I can't rush God and the importance of allowing Him to do things in my life the way He wants to. This lesson on learning what it means to wait took me several years because I continued to try to rush God and tell Him how to fix it.

My waiting experience would have been less painful if I would have chosen to wait with anticipation that God was working our situation out for our good (Romans 8:28).

> **28** *And we know that all things work together for good to them that love God, to them who are the called according to his purpose.*

When you have advance warning that you are on the brink of your breakthrough or that God is going to answer your prayer requests, you should wait with excitement and anticipation, knowing that your answer is on the way. That in God's timing, you will see the manifestation of what you are waiting for. However, if you choose to be hard-headed like I was, you will miss the blessing of waiting! You may ask how is there a blessing in waiting for your prayers to be answered and you are in need now? Well, look at it from this perspective, think back to the child that asks his parent for a toy. When the parent said wait, the child could have chosen to get excited about the fact that the toy was coming! He may not have known exactly when, but if he trusted what his parent said, he would know that it was coming. Therefore, he could have relaxed, and went about his day knowing that he would eventually get his toy! This is how we as believers should respond. When our prayers and requests are in alignment with God's word and His will for our lives, we can ask whatsoever we will in Jesus name knowing that He will do it (John 14:13-14).

> *13 And whatsoever ye shall ask in my name, that will I do, that the Father may be glorified in the Son. 14 If ye shall ask anything in my name, I will do it.*

Getting excited about what you are expecting God to do in your life will prompt you to serve others while you are waiting. Serving others enhances your ability to wait in peace, but also assists others while they may be waiting. We have been taught for far too long that waiting means to hold on until, but choosing to wait on others during your time of waiting is so beneficial (Luke 6:38).

> *38 Give, and it shall be given unto you; good measure, pressed down, and shaken together, and running over, shall men give into your bosom. For with the same measure that ye mete withal it shall be measured to you again.*

It helps to get your mind off of your issues and burdens as well as what you are going through. Waiting on other people has a way of shifting your mindset from "me, me, me" to "How can I serve you?" When you look around to identify who you can help, you will find that there are so many others that are in a far worse situation than what you could ever dream of experiencing. It always helps me to press through my issues when I focus on waiting on others, rather than dwelling on my problems (1 Peter 4:10).

> *10 God has given each of you a gift from his great variety of spiritual gifts. Use them well to serve one another.*

God desires that we serve others while we wait. So what does it mean to wait? It means to love God enough to trust that He is a promise keeper, and when He makes a promise He will uphold His end of the deal (2 Corinthian 1:20)

> ***20** For all of God's promises have been fulfilled in Christ with a resounding "Yes!" And through Christ, our "Amen" (which means "Yes") ascends to God for his glory.*

Every promise in the book belongs to you, and although you may have to wait for it, wait with expectation while serving others. He will honor your faithfulness, and bless you more than you can ever ask or think (Ephesians 3:20).

> ***20** Now all glory to God, who is able, through his mighty power at work within us, to accomplish infinitely more than we might ask or think.*

Prophetic Message

Even since the beginning of time, people have asked many questions about millions of things. Then they try to put their individual spin on what they feel that the definition is, depending on their intellect or education or even on their own self analysis. People say well, no it is (a) no it is (b) no it is (c), and not that they are looking to the great "I Am", to define the answer. It is because they are going on what sounds good in their ears, and what is acceptable to the majority of the response of mankind. But if you want a true definition of what it means to wait, go back to the word. There are things that even I have had to wait on. Even though I had the authority and the power, and the ability to change my situation, I waited, because I knew that it was more than about me.

The definition of being able to wait is "Being able to understand it is not always about you, but it is about some situations you may have to go back and change in your past, some situations that have not even come to you yet in the future, and some situations in the right now." But in order for you to change, it is necessary for you to wait, because if you do not wait you have the tendency, as a man in the flesh, to run head first, just like a fireman in a burning building, not giving any thoughts to what you need to do, which is operating on adrenaline. But in this walk, you cannot and you should not afford to operate on adrenaline. Because think about it, oftentimes when mankind is operating under the influence of adrenaline, they are not thinking logically. In order for you to move in the Spirit, in order for you to truly wait, you must put yourself in a place that you are not operating in self, you are not operating on emotions, and you are not operating on adrenaline, but you are moving, you are speaking, you are hearing, by the directions and the instructions of the Almighty God has spoken and given to you by the Holy Spirit. See it is the Holy Spirit that gives you your strength, gives you the power, and the staying power to be able to wait. No matter how hard it is sometimes you want to grit your teeth because you want to move so badly, but it is the Holy Spirit, that as you call out for me to give you what you need, to be able to stay in that waiting place. If you call on Me, I will answer you, and I will give you everything that you need: that staying power. See it is that staying power that you are going to need to be able to wait because you alone can not do it. No matter how much you try to convince yourself that I am going to stay right here, and I am not going to move, the flesh rises up, and there is a war, a struggle between the flesh and the Spirit. Oftentimes if you do not submit to the true will of God, and the flesh wears out, and then you will decide that you are going to move from that place of waiting. So the true definition of waiting, is being able to hear the Holy Spirit when He is speaking and trusting Him enough to say "When I do not hear Him and He has not given me any instructions to go anywhere, to do anything, or say anything, I will stay right here and wait until He speaks the next instructions." That is the definition of waiting in the Spirit.

What Does It Mean To Wait - Define Waiting

Chapter 4 — Notes

What Are You Waiting For?

Chapter 5

Now that you know what it means to wait, it is more important to know what you are waiting for. Knowing what you are waiting for is not the same as knowing why you are waiting. You may be waiting for a new job, someone new, the newest accessories, a renewed relationship, a healing, a promotion, a business, your deliverance, and the list goes on and on. People wait for all kinds of things, and some of those things require more waiting than others. When you are in a place of waiting, you need to be clear on what you are waiting on and for.

Just like we wait in expectation, for the sun to rise every morning and set every evening, so should we wait for that blessing, that miracle, that breakthrough, or for that situation to change. You must wait for that broken relationship to be restored, that prodigal son to return home, or that frustrating job to be renewed. Whatever you are waiting on, expect it to come to pass and it will happen! You do not lay in bed and think I am going to stop waiting on the sun today, because it is not going to shine today. You expect the sun to rise today, and you wait for it expecting new mercies each day (Lamentations 3: 22-23).

> **22** *The faithful love of the Lord never ends! His mercies never cease.* **23** *Great is his faithfulness; his mercies begin afresh each morning.*

I am grateful that God's mercies are new daily because there were so many days I wanted to give up on waiting. I knew God said that if I was willing to surrender my marriage to Him, He would restore it, but He did not say how long it would take. I did not mind releasing my marital issues to Him, I trusted Him, but the wait felt very long and lonely. Like many of you, I questioned my faith many nights, and I wondered if I had missed God's instructions. I fasted and prayed, and spent quality time in His presence, but the answer I was waiting for seemed so far away. But God in His loving way would always remind me, that He was still with me, and would never leave me nor disappoint me (Hebrews 13:5).

> *5 Don't love money; be satisfied with what you have. For God has said, "I will never fail you. I will never abandon you."*

When I was waiting, He continuously confirmed His promises that if I would wait, He would restore everything that I lost (Deuteronomy 30:3-13).

> *3 then the Lord your God will restore your fortunes. He will have mercy on you and gather you back from all the nations where he has scattered you. 4 Even though you are banished to the ends of the earth, the Lord your God will gather you from there and bring you back again. 5 The Lord your God will return you to the land that belonged to your ancestors, and you will possess that land again. Then he will make you even more prosperous and numerous than your ancestors!*
> *6 "The Lord your God will change your heart and the hearts of all your descen-*

dants, so that you will love him with all your heart and soul and so you may live! 7 The Lord your God will inflict all these curses on your enemies and on those who hate and persecute you. 8 Then you will again obey the Lord and keep all his commands that I am giving you today.
9 "The Lord your God will then make you successful in everything you do. He will give you many children and numerous livestock, and he will cause your fields to produce abundant harvests, for the Lord will again delight in being good to you as he was to your ancestors. 10 The Lord your God will delight in you if you obey his voice and keep the commands and decrees written in this Book of Instruction, and if you turn to the Lord your God with all your heart and soul.
11 "This command I am giving you today is not too difficult for you, and it is not beyond your reach. 12 It is not kept in heaven, so distant that you must ask, 'Who will go up to heaven and bring it down so we can hear it and obey?' 13 It is not kept beyond the sea, so far away that you must ask, 'Who will cross the sea to bring it to us so we can hear it and obey?'

It does not matter what you are waiting on, if God says that He will fix it, He will do just that. He can heal, deliver and set free any situation. My friend was diagnosed with brain cancer last year, and she had to make a decision about what it is she was waiting on. Was she waiting for her doctors to schedule her chemotherapy appointments, an opportunity to break the news to her family, time to see how things will turn out or was she waiting on God to manifest His glory through her total healing? She could have chosen any of these options, and each of them required waiting. The outcome of her diagnosis was dependent upon her knowing what decision to make in this season of her life. I am sure she pondered for a while about her options prior to making a decision, which is natural. She chose to wait on God for her total healing. She reminded God of His promises to heal her physically, and with that decision, it required a "yes" from her spirit!

Today, my friend says that "I still say "yes" to God although some days her "yes" is not as loud as other days. Some days you are in a place where you are stuck because you are not moving forward, but there is no complacency in God. We are either moving forward or backward. There is no standing still because time is yet moving. You may think in your mind that you are standing still, but you are moving. Just know that God is at the end of the process, and He is worth waiting on and for.
That situation that you are waiting for or that person you are waiting on may seem out of reach, but there is nothing too hard for God. He has proven Himself faithful throughout the Bible, and He will not stop healing, delivering, and restoring now. He desires to meet and surpass our needs, we only need to delight ourselves in Him (Psalm 37:4).

> *4 Delight thyself also in the Lord: and he shall give thee the desires of thine heart, and He will and give us the desires of our hearts.*

If your heart's desire is healing, He will do it. If your heart's desire is a degree, He will make a way. If your heart's desire is a renewed relationship, He will restore it. But remember He said that you must delight yourself in Him.

If you desire your marriage to be restored, are you waiting on God to do it, or are you distracted by other people of interest? Waiting for restoration to manifest, spend that quiet time with Him getting to know Him better, and learn what He has in store for you in this season of waiting. If you truly want the restoration to occur, you must be willing to do what is necessary for it to come to pass, and that is waiting. What are you waiting for? You are waiting on God to give you instructions on what and how to wait. Too often, we say we want things to change in our marriage, on our jobs, in our business and so forth, but our lifestyles do not align with what the word says for us to do while we wait. When we wait upon the Lord he will renew our strength (Isaiah 40:31).

> *31 But they that wait upon the Lord shall renew their strength; they shall mount up with wings as eagles; they shall run, and not be weary; and they shall walk, and not faint.*

There are no boundaries on what we wait for, we are just required to wait. Are you willing to wait for what you truly want?

You cannot wait as long as things are looking like they are working in your favor. You only need be concerned with the fact that if you wait, God will come through. You may feel that your financial breakthrough is near, and your husband or wife is near. Are you being a good steward of your current finances, are you preparing yourself to be a husband or wife? Are you willing to wait for it? Speak those things into existence as you are going through the process of waiting. Faith without action is of no avail (James 2: 14-26).

14 *What good is it, dear brothers and sisters, if you say you have faith but don't show it by your actions? Can that kind of faith save anyone?* *15* *Suppose you see a brother or sister who has no food or clothing,* *16* *and you say, "Good-bye and have a good day; stay warm and eat well"—but then you don't give that person any food or clothing. What good does that do?*
17 *So you see, faith by itself isn't enough. Unless it produces good deeds, it is dead and useless.* *18* *Now someone may argue, "Some people have faith; others have good deeds." But I say, "How can you show me your faith if you don't have good deeds? I will show you my faith by my good deeds."* *19* *You say you have faith, for you believe that there is one God. Good for you! Even the demons believe this, and they tremble in terror.* *20* *How foolish! Can't you see that faith without good deeds is useless?* *21* *Don't you remember that our ancestor Abraham was shown to be right with God by his actions when he offered his son Isaac on the altar?* *22* *You see, his faith and his actions worked together. His actions made his faith complete.* *23* *And so it happened just as the Scriptures say: "Abraham believed God, and God counted him as righteous because of his faith." He was even called the friend of God.* *24* *So you see, we are shown to be right with God by what we do, not by faith alone.* *25* *Rahab the prostitute is another example. She was shown to be right with God by her ac-*

> *tions when she hid those messengers and sent them safely away by a different road. **26** Just as the body is dead without breath, so also faith is dead without good works.*

Begin to decree that your finances are restored, your marriage is renewed, your children are respectful. Whatever you are waiting for, believe that you have it, and it shall be established (Proverbs 16:3).

> ***3** Commit your actions to the Lord, and your plans will succeed.*

I was waiting for restoration in my marriage, and I failed the test miserably at first and had to retake it. I was selfish and wanted God to fix things the way I wanted him to do it, and I wanted it right then. It did not take me long to realize that God is not the author of confusion and He operates in a Spirit of Excellence. Once I took on the mind of Christ and acknowledged Him as Lord over my life and situation, things started to change on my behalf (Romans 12:1-2).

> ***1-2** So here's what I want you to do, God helping you: Take your everyday, ordinary life—your sleeping, eating, going-to-work, and walking-around life—and place it before God as an offering. Embracing what God does for you is the best thing you can do for him. Don't become so well-adjusted to your culture that you fit into it without even thinking. Instead, fix your attention on God. You'll be changed from the inside out. Readily recognize what he wants from you, and*

quickly respond to it. Unlike the culture around you, always dragging you down to its level of immaturity, God brings the best out of you, develops well-formed maturity in you.

    I had to determine what I was actually waiting for, and how He desires that I wait. That lesson has taken me far in my journey, and I now know that it is important to know what I am waiting for and wait regardless of the length of time. Because if God said that He will do it, He will do just what He said that He will do!

Prophetic Message

This is an individual question, and even though there are many people reading this book, and some of you are even reading it as a group study, it is still an individual question that only you can answer. There are some of you that may feel like you know what you are waiting on, but then as life's circumstances start to unfold you begin to think about and experience uncertainties concerning that situation or that person that you are waiting on. Is it really for you, or is it because you see your surroundings and see that it applies to others? Is that really what you want? It is at this time you must put yourself in a place of solitude so that you can take note.

Do a self-examination and not only ask yourself what am I waiting on, but ask yourself why am I waiting for it? It is through this process that you are going to find out that some of the things that you feel you are waiting on do not even necessarily apply to you. Not in the place that you are, and not in the place that you need to be. See in this place, the question that you are asking, may not necessarily apply to the "old you" where you used to be, but it doesn't necessarily answer the question about the "new you" that you are trying to transform and conform into for where God is taking you either. You must understand that in this process if you are asking this question about what it is that you are waiting on, you must ask yourself "Am I waiting on this question to be answered because of selfish gain, because of self notoriety", or "Am I waiting on this question to be answered because I truly want to walk in the calling that God has created and the purpose for which He has made me". Once you answer this question, you will understand what it is you are waiting for. You may find that those things or that person you thought you were waiting around for at this point in time, or that relationship you are waiting to change is actually insignificant. You may also find that the person really does not fit into the puzzle that God is trying to complete in this particular season of your spiritual growth.

Make a list and ask God about it, and then ask yourself how is this situation or this person going to benefit the kingdom, and how is it going to benefit fulfilling His purpose for you? When you ask to hear from God and He responds to you, you will find that when you get to the end of your list, you will have your top three (3) things that you are waiting on. Once God has defined that these are the top three things you are waiting for, you should get excited now that it is clear. There are some of you that although you have been waiting a long time know that it's getting close. You are on the brink of your breakthrough, and that's why you lack patience and are frustrated. This is what you are waiting for. Focus on those things, saith God, and you will be successful in your spiritual growth.

What Are You Waiting For?

Chapter 5 — Notes

What Are You Waiting For?   While I Wait

The Importance of Waiting - Why Should We Wait

Chapter 6

It is important to wait for God to answer your request, because it proves your level of trust towards Him. You must get to a place in your life that you are confident in saying "I will wait until" and realize that "until" is when God does it. You have to acknowledge that He knows what is best for you and that He has the time set to answer every prayer you have before Him, but you cannot waver in your waiting. Is it worth it to you to wait as long as it takes for the answer to manifest itself? Your wait may be instantaneous, a few minutes, a few hours, a few days, a few weeks, a few months, and for some it may take years. While you wait, no matter how long it takes for the answer, trust the process knowing that He is working things out for your good (Romans 8:26-28).

> *26-28 Meanwhile, the moment we get tired in the waiting, God's Spirit is right alongside helping us along. If we don't know how or what to pray, it doesn't matter. He does our praying in and for us, making prayer out of our wordless sighs, our aching groans. He knows us far better than we know ourselves, knows our pregnant condition, and keeps us present before God. That's why we can be so sure that every detail in our lives of love for God is worked into something good.*

When I first accepted Christ in my life I could pray for something and it seemed like I received my answers before I could release them into the atmosphere. Talk about a new level of excitement for this new believer. I was so excited I would try to find just about anything to pray about just so I could experience how quickly God moved on my behalf. Of course, I eventually realized that not all prayers are answered immediately, but that does not mean that God has forgotten nor that He is not going to answer. I learned that He knew what I needed that season of my life, and He knows about you as well. He is an on time God and will answer immediately if need be.

As time passed, I learned to depend on His timing more than my need. I used to get so upset when I did not have enough money to pay my bills because I was so accustomed to paying them on time. But I learned a valuable lesson over the years, in that the blessings of the Lord makes one rich and adds no sorrow (Proverbs 10:22).

22 The blessing of the Lord makes a person rich, and he adds no sorrow with it.

When I realized that it is all God who provides for me, and blesses me, I stopped struggling with waiting for Him to answer. I trust Him to take care of all of my needs and desires, therefore, if the answer does not come immediately I am fine with it because I know it will eventually come.

After my divorce, I was able to continue managing our household with ease for a while, but then came a season of drought. During this time of drought, I was faced with a time of waiting for over three years. I was no longer able to pay my bills or manage my finances. Not only was I experiencing loneliness in my relationship with Eric, but also with God. I knew He was there, but He was very quiet. I knew that He loved me and He cared about my well-being, but I could not help but wonder had He forgotten me. I could not pay my mortgage, and the collection calls kept coming. I did what I knew best to do, and that was to continue to wait on God to see me through my storm and manifest His glory through it. After three years of me not making a house payment, God turned my situation around, worked my mortgage out for my good. We are still in our home, and I am grateful to Him. I experienced God in a new way, and He taught me the importance of waiting on Him, and not leaning to my own understanding because I could not see my way out of my situation in the natural (Proverbs 3:5-6).

> *5 Trust in the Lord with all your heart; do not depend on your own understanding. 6 Seek his will in all you do, and he will show you which path to take.*

I knew that He did not bless me with my home to lose it, and He did just that.

Your back may be up against the wall, and you may not see any way out, but if you will continue to trust God knowing that He knows the end from the beginning and He will never leave you nor forsake you (Hebrews 13:5-6).

> *5-6 Don't be obsessed with getting more material things. Be relaxed with what you have. Since God assured us, "I'll never let you down, never walk off and leave you," we can boldly quote, God is there, ready to help; I'm fearless no matter what. Who or what can get to me?*

It is so important to wait on God, because what if I had given up on waiting for Him to rescue me with my mortgage situation. How many people do you know that can literally be strapped and not pay their mortgage for over thirty-six months and walk away with that home without penalty. That is the kind of God we serve. He wants us to have and live a balanced life, and when we are faced with adversities, if we will surrender our cares to Him, He will take what the devil means for our bad and work it out for our good. So, fear not if you are in a place of waiting for Him to answer you. He is faithful and just to do just that. He loves you and He knows what you need before you ask Him, but are you willing to wait for Him to answer?

It is easy to get ahead of God when we are not in total fellowship with Him, or if He takes too long to answer us. We get antsy when He does not answer quickly, and start listening to our flesh. That voice eventually consumes our thoughts and guides our actions. It is better to cast those thoughts down at onset and press in more to hear what God is saying (2 Corinthians 10:3-6).

> *3 For though we walk in the flesh, we do not war after the flesh: 4 (For the weapons of our warfare are not carnal, but mighty through God to the pulling down of strong holds;) 5 Casting down imaginations, and every high thing that exalteth itself against the knowledge of God, and bringing into captivity every thought to the obedience of Christ; 6 And having in a readiness to revenge all disobedience, when your obedience is fulfilled.*

It is important to wait on Him no matter how long it takes for Him to answer. The important factor is knowing that He is going to answer and that He will do what is best for you.

To wait on God is a decision and not a feeling. It is important to push past your feelings and wait on Him to perform that miracle, to meet that need, to save that loved one, and to answer that prayer. Your decision to wait has to be an agreement to wait as long as it takes. Do not get weary in waiting, because at the right time you will receive whatever you are waiting for (Galatians 6:9).

> *9 So let's not get tired of doing what is good. At just the right time we will reap a harvest of blessing if we don't give up.*

Prophetic Message

When it comes to the word "time", God says "I often sit back and laugh when it applies to man." Because as I (Jesus) sit on the right hand of my father, and I watch mankind on a daily basis, man's life is often driven by time. You have those that say "I have certain things that I must accomplish in a certain period of time". You have those that refer to what they consider a bucket list they want to complete before the end of time. You have those that are striving for certain areas of their life that they have to complete at particular times. But this all to me is a joke as I look at mankind because God is the one and the only one that can define time. He is time. Without God, time does not exist. Whether it is a short period of time, whether it is a few seconds, whether it is a few minutes, whether it is a few hours, or a few days, or a few years, they all look the same to Him because He is time. He spoke in the beginning and there was time. Every day that He is speaking, there is time. Even after He gives you all of the time, God says, "What are you doing with the time?" He says, that He often hears mankind say that there are not enough hours in the day, but the question is out of these hours in the day, how much time do you spend in fellowship with Him. He is time.

Oh, you have a character that you refer to as "Father Time", but God is time, and when He comes back, His word says that time will be no more. So that should tell you and should help you understand that He holds time in the very word, in His very breath, in His very presence is time. So I say to you do not ask the question about how long you should wait, as far as time is concerned. Rather in my waiting period how much time am I dedicating and am I giving to you? If you are asking this question and you are giving me all of the time "Father Time" belongs to me anyway. It is because He is such a loving God that He allows you the time in order to be able to complete the tasks that you need to do. It is because He understands as a loving God that this is necessary because you live in the world. Therefore, time is essential, but more importantly the essential time of the world is the time to complete your individual assignments. Understanding that time is not important to God as it is to you. So why is time so important to you, especially if you are not doing what God has assigned you to do. The answer to how long should I wait is answered when you are doing what God tells you to do! Your waiting period is going to seem insignificant once you complete the assignment and you are going to find yourself asking the question "Was it that long?" It is because your focus is not necessarily on time itself, but your focus is on the giver and the holder of time. Focus on Him says God, the giver of time and then you will not even have to worry about how long you need to wait. You are going to walk into those things that you have defined, that you are waiting on and you are going to see Him manifest them. Then what you felt was long will not be that long a period of time, because you recognize the giver, and the creator, and the one who holds the time.

The Importance of Waiting - Why Should We Wait

Chapter 6 — Notes

Learn How To Wait - How Do You Wait?

Chapter 7

Learning how to wait is a huge task for many, because you only want to wait when you know what the outcome is going to be. It is more difficult to wait when God is quiet, and you do not see an answer in your future. You can choose to take the easy road, which is to give up and move to your next situation or learn the dynamics of how to wait. How does God want us to wait for a blessing, a healing, a breakthrough, a deliverance? He wants you to make Him your priority so that He can teach you how to wait. Once you have a clear understanding of what you are waiting for, there are some action steps that are necessary. The bible says in all of our getting we should get understanding (Proverbs 4:7)

> *7 Wisdom is the principal thing; therefore get wisdom: and with all thy getting get understanding.*

Therefore, learning how to wait requires you to pray, plan, study, and believe that while you wait, these steps will grow you in patience and maturity.

Your first step is to pray for God to order your steps while you wait, because, during this waiting process, it is important for your steps to be ordered by God (Psalm 37:23).

> *23 The steps of a good man are ordered by the LORD: and he delighteth in his way.*

When we attempt to handle our own situations, and life's issues we are asking for bigger trouble. God desires to lead and direct us into the path of righteousness, but He will not force Himself on us. When you pray about your situation and totally trust Him with everything in you depending solely on God to work things out, your waiting becomes bearable (Proverbs 3:5-6).

> *5 Trust in the Lord with all your heart; do not depend on your own understanding. 6 Seek his will in all you do, and he will show you which path to take.*

I found that I had to pray constantly in order to keep my sanity while I waited for God to bring me through my situation. There were times I could only pray "Lord help me", and there were times, I could only cry out His name. Sometimes depending on the intensity of your wait, you have to rely on the Holy Spirit to make intercession on your behalf (Romans 8:26).

> *26 And the Holy Spirit helps us in our weakness. For example, we don't know what God wants us to pray for. But the Holy Spirit prays for us with groanings that cannot be expressed in words.*

However you need to communicate with God, do it so that you can embrace your time of waiting.

The next step is to plan a strategy to use while you wait. This plan should be such that you can visualize your end results. Every time it looks like your situation isn't getting better but worse, revisit your plan. Many times it is necessary to write your plan down and live by that plan during your time of waiting (Habakkuk 2:2)

> *2 And the LORD answered me, and said, Write the vision, and make it plain upon tables, that he may run that readeth it.*

If it helps you to have a visual, use a sticky note and put it on your refrigerator, your bathroom mirror, in your car, on your bedpost or wherever you frequent throughout the day. The plan should include your daily method of operation. What will you do daily while you wait? How will you do it while you wait? When will you do certain things while you wait? Where will you do certain things? Who will be a part of your support team while you wait? All of these questions are important to answer in your plan of action while you wait. If you do not know where you are going, you will probably end up someplace else. When you know what God wants for you while you wait it is easier to plan your strategy.

The third step is to study in order to know what the word says about waiting. It is important to study to show yourself approved unto God (2 Timothy 2:15).

> *15 Work hard so you can present yourself to God and receive his approval. Be a good worker, one who does not need to be ashamed and who correctly explains the word of truth.*

When you study the word, it equips you for every situation that you encounter during your season of waiting. Every instruction that you need to help you endure your wait is found in the word of God. Precept upon precept, line upon line, here a little there a little (Isaiah 28:10).

10 *He tells us everything over and over--
one line at a time, one line at a time, a little
here, and a little there.*

There are a magnitude of self-help books available to you to help you embrace the word of God during your season of waiting. In order to determine the appropriate book for you to read and study, you need to ask yourself "What is it that I am waiting for at this moment?" Then you can find the book that will best meet your needs and help you to endure the hurt, the pain, the frustration, and everything that you are experiencing while you wait.

Learning how to wait was one of the biggest tasks that I have ever endured. I found myself always wanting God to answer my prayers right then, and or at least give me a clue as to what He was doing in my life, and how long I was going to have to wait. But as time passed, I realize that God does not operate like that. I had to learn how to pray, and literally, plan some strategies to use each time I was going through a season of waiting. I found that when I studied His word, shut out all of the distractions, and seek His face, I could hear from Him. It reminds me of the scripture that says

"If my people, which are called by my name, shall humble themselves, and pray, and seek my face, and turn from their wicked ways; then will I hear from heaven, and will forgive their sin, and will heal their land (2 Chronicles 7:14)."

When I turned from my wicked ways of thinking and sought the Lord on how I should wait, I began to experience a level of peace that surpassed my greatest understanding during my season of waiting.

Prophetic Message

The important thing to remember before you answer the question about what you should be doing while you are waiting, is to go back and study what you are waiting for. In these three things that you are studying and what I (God) have defined that you are waiting for, your actions are going to be different in order to get you to the resolution of your waiting period. Your relationship with Me (God) number one, should be fine-tuned because you have been in a place of complacency, where it has no longer been a priority so now while you are waiting, God is your priority.

This is a relationship, so in this relationship, you want to spend more time with Him, intimate time with God, not rushed because we are not in rush hour. You must spend quality time with Him to the point where you are looking forward to spending time with Him because you know that this time that He is going to give you divine instructions. In this relationship and in this quiet time is where He is going to mold you, and in order to do that, this is a part of your purging process. Where He is going to be pulling things out of you and casting them away, and no more to return. In this process, He is going to strengthen you where you are weak. So as you are praying, and for those of you that have your prayer language, use it as you are coming into my presence and you are calling on Him. Sometimes in this place, it is not necessary for you to say anything, because all He needs in this place is just for you to come and let Him pour into you.

It is through this praying and fasting, that He needs you to understand that fasting is not always about what you are putting in your body, but what you are looking at, what you are listening to, and the places that you are going. So in this place, you should be fasting, you should be praying, and building your relationship with me. You should be minimizing those little distractions. You already know what they are because you have tried on many occasions to justify why they are not a distraction. Turn off those televisions, and turn off those radios, and get in that secret place, where you can hear God when He is speaking. Just as simple as when you are coming and you are saying, Lord, I am here speak because your servant heareth.

Listen to Me (God) pouring into you, but I must warn you that in this time and in this process as I am speaking because your spirit is open, your heart is open, your mind is open unto Me, I am going to pour out and pour into you those things you must hold close in your mind, in your heart, and in your spirit. Some of you will get so excited about what it is that I am releasing and what I am showing you that you will want to run and tell others, but I must warn you that it is not the time for you to do that, not in this season of waiting. Later it will be time, but in your season of waiting, it is not the time.

It is integral that the things that He releases unto you that you holdfast and you hold them tight and you meditate and you ponder in your heart because in this place, for My dreamers the visions will be even more vivid and they will be so plain as if you were there. They are of things to come as you come out of your season of waiting. So remember the steps that you should be doing. More importantly, remember there is something that I have given you during this time and in this season of what you should do while you are waiting.

Learn How To Wait - How Do You Wait?

Chapter 7— Notes

The Results Of Waiting   While I Wait

Because I Waited - The Results Of Waiting

Chapter 8

Over my life, there were many times that I've had to wait. Although I wanted my answers right then, I found that because I waited it was worth the wait. My wait did not feel good at the time I was going through the wait, but the end result was truly a blessing. I remember crying like a baby whenever I had to wait after my husband left, but I learned that when I stopped whining and complaining and ranting and raging all over the place, God could hear and answer my prayers. I spent countless hours asking Him why, but I learned that God is not deaf and He loves me and cares.

I thought I was going to be happy once Eric left, but when reality set in I realized that maybe that was not what I wanted to do. Did I really want to have to experience a wait when I did not know how long the wait was going to actually be? I found that there was a process I had to go through and this process helped me to grow through my situation while I waited. Once I got the lesson I was supposed to get from experiencing this wait, the blessing came, which was that God brought us back together! Now I understand not everyone's situation will turn out like our situation, as I stated earlier about the prodigal son. However, there is something or someone that you were waiting on that if you will only put your trust in God and lean not to your own understanding, he will answer that prayer for you (Proverbs 3:5-6).

> *5 Trust in the LORD with all your heart; do not depend on your own understanding. 6 Seek his will in all you do, and he will show you which path to take.*

When you make a decision to wait and you follow through with that wait, there is a great return on your investment. An investment for our purposes is an act of devoting your time, effort, or energy to that situation that you are waiting for with an expectation of receiving a worthwhile return. I treated my marriage as an investment, therefore, my return was positive. Yes, when he left, it hurt during the season of waiting, but the return reminded me of having a child. I was sick for nine months with my youngest baby and literally threw up every single day for nine months. However, on January 2, 2001, when I laid my eyes on her for the very first time, it was well worth every pain I endured, every night I was up and could not get comfortable, and every time I had to call for my husband and son to come and help me. Those nine months seem like they would never come to an end, and it was as though the closer I got to delivery time, the more difficult it was for me to wait. My investment worked in my favor, and allowed me the opportunity to receive blessings beyond anything I could ever ask or even imagine coming to me (Ephesians 3:20).

> *20 Now unto him that is able to do exceeding abundantly above all that we ask or think, according to the power that worketh in us.*

When I understood the biblical principle of reciprocity it helped me in my experiences of having to wait and learning how to wait. I began to receive blessings after blessings after blessings! When situations occur, I wait, then I receive, and the process starts again. A situation happens, I wait, then I receive! I remember going through an experience years ago when I had a full-service T-shirt business. I remember getting audited by the Internal Revenue Service (IRS) and they accused me of not handling my finances in a traditional manner. My parents and my husband financed my business duing that time, and there were a lot of days when it was time for payroll, I literally had to get money from one of the two of them in order to pay my bills. I received the money legitimately from my parents and or my husband, but the IRS was convinced that I must have had some type of illegal business going on. Therefore, I was left owing over $36,000. During that time, I could not even rent a video movie, because that debt ruined my credit. Long story short, I didn't have the money to pay the debt, and yes, I was upset because I knew I did not owe this money. There was a waiting period I had to go through in order for me to grow through this situation. The end result was that because I waited and trusted God to handle the situation for me, even though it was not easy all the time He worked it out on my behalf. I received a letter in the mail years later about an offer in compromise that I forgot I had applied for. The letter came at the most opportune time, and read Paid In Full! I received the return on my investment and received this blessing because I waited on God to handle it for me.

When I learned how to wait, and experienced what happens when I wait, it increased my faith. It prompted me to spend more time in prayer and in the presence of God. I grew closer to Him as a result of the amount of time we spent together. Growing closer to God was actually one of my greatest benefits of waiting. Learning to listen to God for His instructions as to what to do while I wait no matter what it is that I am waiting for was a joy. I found that my experiences of learning how to wait and learning to wait was really designed for me to help someone else who is going through a season of waiting. There are many of you that are experiencing heartaches, headaches, frustration, marital issues, wayward children, to only name a few and you are in that place of waiting for an answer and/or for God to solve the situation for you. He desires for you to wait on him knowing that he will renew your strength (Isaiah 40:31).

> *31 But those who trust in the LORD will find new strength. They will soar high on wings like eagles. They will run and not grow weary. They will walk and not faint.*

You do not have to go through this season of waiting alone, because you are now equipped in what to do while you wait. God has purposed me to help you learn how to wait and learn what to do while you wait. There's nothing like being taught by your experiences, but the greatest lesson is growing through those experiences.

While I was waiting on God during my separation and divorce it also helped me to grow my relationship with God. I had more time to spend with him during my quiet time. That was a great time to study his word and to spend quality time in prayer. Yes, I am sure I could have found many other things that I could be doing while I was waiting, but because I truly wanted to receive that return of my investment, I found that it was the most valuable return I could have ever received. You too can experience such a great return on your investment, when you learn what to do while you wait.

Prophetic Message

My experiences can be compared to that of the prodigal son, because even admittedly sometimes by my own words, I said that I got tired of waiting. As we look at the prodigal son, he too got tired of waiting, even though the very best in the kingdom was his, much silver, much gold, was his. The best of the best was his, even more than he could have ever even imagined was his. But because he got blinded and tripped up by what he saw, he decided that he wanted it right then and there. I am not a microwave God. Only when it is necessary, I can move quickly. But those things that you are asking did not require a quick response or quick action.

Oftentimes in the human body and in the human mind, you want things done instantly like a microwave. You want the situation to be that you push a button and it is done. But what is to be learned in the process of instantaneous? What kind of refining process is this? How can you spiritually grow if everything is instantaneous? What does that teach you about the longevity of the Christian walk, if everything is instantaneous? That is why it is important to learn how to wait in the process. Because once you have an expectation of something, it develops a pattern. The pattern is if He fixes it fast this time, you want it quick the next time, but there is no grounding in fixing it fast because you tend to operate on emotions. There is no molding of the heart when it is fixed fast. There is no maturity growth when it's fixed fast. There is no conforming and transforming your mind and spirit when it is fixed fast. That is why when you get in the place to wait you do not want to find yourself in a place like the prodigal son because every story may not end with a happy ending as that did of the prodigal son.

The word says "He came to himself." Sometimes when you get outside the will of God it is hard for you to come to yourself because you have allowed self to take over and to make decisions. You are listening only to the mind of reason and logic of self, and there is no room for the Holy Spirit to give you instructions. So why not save yourself a lot of trouble and you do not even have to worry about coming to yourself. My question to you is "What is the harm in waiting"? Has God not proved Himself to be a just God. Has He not proved Himself to be a loving God? Has He not done everything that He said that He would do? Look, as the birds fly do I not feed them, as the rain comes does it not water the earth, do the flowers not grow. So God has not changed, He is the same and that is important if you do not want to find yourself in a prodigal son situation where the possibility is that you may not be able to come to yourself and return home to the father and claim your victory that was yours in the very beginning, by not waiting to get everything that He has promised you. When you know that it is coming, why not wait? That is God's question to you, why not wait on the Lord?

Because I Waited - The Results Of Waiting

Chapter 8— Notes

The Results Of Waiting   While I Wait

Waiting Pitfalls - The Downward Spiral

Chapter 9

It is always a good thing to wait when you are in a season of waiting, however, there are consequences when we choose not to wait. The consequences of not waiting can result in failure of getting the answers to your prayers. It is so much easier when we choose to wait, but God is a God who gives you options. If the option you choose is not to wait, then do not get upset when you experience failure in your situation. I could not understand why I was not experiencing success when I was in a season of waiting, but it did not take me long to learn that when I did not follow the instructions that I was given by God, and when I get ahead of him I always run into a roadblock.

Another consequence you will experience when you choose not to wait is risking the chance of making a mistake. When you are doing your own thing, living your own life, and not waiting on God, you can do the wrong thing. What does that look like? It literally means that you are operating in your own strength and you are making a decision that may not be the decision that God has prepared for you. He has a plan and He has a purpose for every step of your life and when you fail to heed to His instructions, a mistake is likely to happen.

I am a prime example of what happens when you choose not to wait on the move of God. I moved ahead of God when I should have waited for Him to change things in my marriage, and it cost me the marriage. That was a grave mistake I made, and I had to go through because of my disobedience to listening to the instructions that God gave me. If I had waited until he answered my prayers, things may have been different. It worked out in my favor, but there were still consequences I had to endure because of my disobedience. So yes, God can still honor our situations when we make a mess of things, but it will be so much better if we listen to His instructions, and do what He asks us to do from the beginning. The consequences of me not waiting resulted in me having to go through a time of loneliness, disappointment, embarrassment, and singleness for a longer period than I would have if only I waited. If you are in a season of waiting and you are trying to make a decision as to whether or not you are going to wait on God, take it from someone who has been there and done that, it is so much more beneficial to wait.

Some consequences we face as a result of being disobedient to God by choosing not to wait, can have life-altering outcomes. These outcomes can have irrevocable consequences, and leave lasting scars. How many times have you regretted not waiting for a situation to happen in your life, only to find out that you made matters worse? David experienced consequences for getting ahead of God and suffered some irrevocable results. When he changed his thinking, he humbled himself and waited patiently upon the Lord and He shall incline to him and heard his cry (Psalm 40:1).

> *1 I waited patiently for the LORD to help me, and he turned to me and heard my cry.*

That is a great place to be in as a matter fact, because when we can humble ourselves after we have messed up, God can use that situation and take what the devil meant for our bad and work it out for our good (Genesis 50:20).

> *20 You intended to harm me, but God intended it all for good. He brought me to this position so I could save the lives of many people.*

Yes, there were consequences that followed his mistakes and him getting ahead of God, but he did not stay there. He laid before God and asked God to create in him a clean heart and renew the right spirit that was within him (Psalm 51:10).

> *10 Create in me a clean heart, O God; and renew a right spirit within me.*

The sad part about all of this is that sometimes you cannot fix what is broken. You can correct your behavior and do better, but once the damage is done it is done. You just have to change your mind (repent), pick up the pieces, and move forward from that point.

Another consequence of not waiting for God is to miss the blessing or opportunity. You think that things are going to work out in your favor, and you wonder later what happened. When you do not listen to God's specific instructions on waiting, you risk having a missed opportunity. It is not worth missing the move of God in your life because you are impatient. There are always pitfalls and warning signs that you should watch out for when you are in a season of waiting. If you find that the person or situation you are waiting on is taking a long time to manifest, ask yourself "Did I miss the warning signs"? There will always be warning signs that send messages to you to prompt you to refocus when you are approaching a pitfall. Some common warnings signs to avoid while you wait are: danger ahead - watch out, don't do it - you are making a big mistake, stop and plan - you have not planned your situation properly, don't miss God - you are about to miss the move of God, stand still - a missed opportunity ahead, or just wait.

The final consequence of not waiting on God that is critical is missing the timing of God. You do not want to miss God's timing. Timing with God is everything because His time is not our time, His thoughts are not our thoughts, and His ways are not our ways (Isaiah 55:8-9).

***8** For my thoughts are not your thoughts, neither are your ways my ways, declares the Lord. **9** As the heavens are higher than the earth, so are my ways higher than your ways and my thoughts than your thoughts.*

Too often you get complacent thinking that you have all the time in the world, or that you are running out of time, but God wants you to know that everything is within His timing. When you fail to wait on God and His timing, you risk the chance of missing what He has for you. What he has for you is so much more important than you desiring to get ahead of Him or you wanting to rush Him. It is better to stand still and wait no matter how long it takes rather than running ahead of God and missing the blessing that He has purposed for your life.

I almost missed the timing of God during the time of my divorce. I met a gentleman that became a great telephone friend, and we spent a lot of time together working his ministry and helping him fulfill his purpose and his destiny. I believe God connected us for that season so that he could advance to his next dimension in ministry, but because we spent so much time together, I lost focus. I do not have any regrets about helping him or about spending the countless months building a relationship that was not destined by God, but I almost missed God. I was experiencing the hurt of being divorced, and I gave up hope of ever thinking that Eric and I would reunite. I began to focus on the possibility of uniting with this man and starting a ministry together. All of that sounds great, right? But that was not what God had in mind for us. God had a different plan for my life, and if I did not have prayer warriors praying for me I would have moved ahead of God, and probably married the wrong person. I would have missed my opportunity to reunite with my husband and my story would be a lot different today.

You cannot base what our situation looks like or feels like on where you are going, because your end results can look very different from our now. God has a plan and a purpose for your life and He desires that you walk in obedience to Him and His word (Jeremiah 29:11).

> *11 For I know the plans I have for you, says the LORD. They are plans for good and not for disaster, to give you a future and a hope.*

When you fail to wait on the move of God and the blessings of God you are more apt to suffer the consequences that follow. Do not be weary in well doing , and don't get discouraged when the wait takes longer than you expect (Galatians 6:9).

> *9 So let's not get tired of doing what is good. At just the right time we will reap a harvest of blessing if we don't give up.*

Just know that He will send you warnings to remind you that He desires that you wait, but if you choose not to wait there will be consequences.

Prophetic Message

How many times have you found yourself in an uncomfortable situation because of a decision you made out of haste? You decided that God was taking too long to come or when He came and gave you the answer, it wasn't the answer you wanted. You pray and ask God for help, and say that you trust Him, but you don't. You question His decision when He gives you the answer, but you cannot have it both ways. Either you are going to ask and believe, or you are going to choose your own answer. It is the answer that's in His divine will, that you should apply to your situation. It is important that you listen, and be willing to accept the answer, and not operate in your own thinking by moving ahead like a locomotive. Some of you are like locomotives, because once the train leaves the station it is full speed ahead and you do not take time to back up and to wait. You say "Now is this really the answer that God is giving me or is it me operating on my own thoughts and my own emotions" ?

You will find in many of your situations that emotions have no foundations, and they change just like the wind changes. But you must wait patiently because some of you have no patience. You want an answer right then, and it costs you to have to go back and do it all over again. This is the hamster effect. You are on that wheel and you can't get off. You hear the pitter-patter of your feet as the hamster on that wheel. You hear the wheel going round and round, and as you look around you see that you have not accomplished hardly anything. As a matter of fact, you have wasted valuable and precious time that you could have spent just waiting and listening for divine instructions. Once you get in the habit of waiting, and listening, and looking, and opening up to receive divine instructions, you will find that it was not as hard as you thought it was had you not decided to go out and get ahead of Him. It is a dangerous thing when you are in a relationship with Christ, yet try to get ahead of Him and His thinking, and in His planning, and in the implementing of what His plan is. It is a dangerous thing to get out of the will of God. It is safe in that place because His safety gives you a security with a hedge of protection in that place of waiting. You will know that when He comes to get you out of that place of waiting, you are not even going to worry about how long you were there because you are going to be doing what He has instructed you to do so wait in the place of safety.

Waiting Pitfalls - The Downward Spiral

Chapter 9— Notes

How Do You Wait? - A Call To Action

Chapter 10

Now that you have learned that it is important to wait, the benefits of waiting, what you should do while you wait, and that there are consequences when you choose not to wait, the question becomes how do you wait? There are specific steps and a process to how you wait. It is important to know this process in order to avoid having to experience that same season of waiting over and over again. While you wait, there can be a lot of anxiety, but if you learn how to wait, the level of anxiety will be less stressful. So let's talk about how do you wait.

The first step in understanding how to wait is to literally do something while you wait. You cannot sit still and expect change to come when you are not doing anything in order for the change to take place. You must be actively engaged in everyday life while you wait. You must continue to stay focused on your job, your relationships, your home, your ministry, your community, and everything that concerns you while you wait. There is a scripture that says whatever your hands find to do, do it well because there is no work after death (Ecclesiastes 9:10).

> *10 Whatever your hand finds to do, do it with all your might, for in the realm of the dead, where you are going, there is neither working nor planning nor knowledge nor wisdom.*

Just because you are waiting for your blessing to manifest itself in the natural it does not mean that you are doing nothing. It means that you are actively pursuing life or living life to the fullest while you wait.

I experienced a season where I felt lost for over three and a half years immediately following the death of my mother. I was waiting on God to explain to me why my prayers were not answered concerning her. I went through a season of being angry, being frustrated, being unclear, and just not knowing whether I wanted to keep going. While I was waiting and going through this tough grieving season, it wasn't until I grabbed hold to the fact that waiting for Him to answer me did not mean for me to close myself up in my bedroom. It meant for me to continue living, to continue helping other people, and to continue working my ministries. When I realized that God was waiting on me to live when I thought I was waiting on Him, it made all the difference in my approach to waiting. In other words, it was important how I waited. Therefore, while you wait, keep on working, keep on praying, keep on believing, keep on doing everything that is required of you while you wait.

Secondly, you must wait in prayer. What does that look like? While you wait you should praying in season and out of season (1 Thessalonians 5:17).

17 Never stop praying.

In other words, you should be seeking the face of God continuously to receive clear instructions on what He desires for you to do while you wait. He is clear about His purpose for your life, but without prayer and seeking him in reference to the steps to take, it makes your wait more difficult. Prayer is the key to unlocking your faith while you wait. Your faith will take you through the process but prayer will help you to endure the process.

The next step is to have a positive attitude while you wait. It is important to refrain from murmuring and complaining while you wait. Your attitude will determine your altitude when your season of waiting comes to an end. God desires that we are thankful in all things (1 Thessalonians 5:18).

> *18 Be thankful in all circumstances, for this is God's will for you who belong to Christ Jesus.*

That does not mean that you love everything that is going on in your life, nor does it mean that you are satisfied with the trial that you are enduring. It means you must have a thankful heart to God that your situation is no worse than it is. You must realize that there is someone else who is going through a situation far worse than you could ever think or imagine going through. When you look at it from someone else's perspective you will realize that what you are going through is nothing compared to the next person. So be grateful, and excited about where God is taking you when you get to the other side of your wait. That is how you wait.

The final step needed when learning how to wait is having faith. Faith is a key component to believing that whatever you are going through will not last always. Faith will keep you from losing your mind when it looks like God has forgotten. When your season of waiting goes for days, weeks, months, and for some years, having faith the size of a mustard seed will keep your mind stayed on him. Never let doubt creep into your mind and cause you to waver in your faith.

I will admit that my faith wavered when I was waiting on God to move in my marriage, and again when I was waiting on God to move on behalf of my son. It was as though God became totally silent when my son was trying to find his way and making some decisions that were not in his best interest. I felt like my world was falling apart and I didn't know how to put it back together again. But deep down inside my spirit, I grabbed what little faith I could find, and I believed for a change with every fiber of my being. I was like David in the bible when he said I would have fainted unless I believe to see the goodness of God in the land of the living. I waited on God and was of a good courage, and He strengthened my heart (Psalm 27:13-14).

> ***13** I had fainted, unless I had believed to see the goodness of the Lord in the land of the living. **14** Wait on the Lord: be of good courage, and he shall strengthen thine heart: wait, I say, on the Lord.*

It pays to wait on Him. Where there is breath, there is hope, and where there is hope, there is life. I found hope in my faith, and the rays from the SON started shining through to give me a spirit of peace while I was waiting.

Learning the steps of how to wait is necessary while you wait. Knowing how to wait can save you a lot of time, frustration, and heartache. The time that is lost in worrying, whining, complaining, and telling other people that cannot help you get out of the situation any quicker is not worth the heartache that follows. The frustration you experience leads to deeper issues when you try to handle things on your own. It is in your best interest to apply the action steps while you wait. When you know that you should keep working while you wait, stay in constant prayer while you wait, keep a positive attitude while you wait, and never let go of your faith while you wait, it will make your time of waiting so much easier to endure. Hold fast to your faith knowing that God knows everything about you and He cares about what happens to you (Hebrews 10:23).

> *23 Let us hold fast the profession of our faith without wavering; for he is faithful that promised.*

Therefore, when you apply those steps on how to wait you will experience the Prince of Peace while you wait.

Prophetic Message

When a child is born, and he comes into this world, everything that child is going to know is learned. He has to learn how to eat, he has to learn what to eat, he has to learn how to walk, he has to learn how to talk, he has to learn about danger, and he has to learn about safety. He has to learn what is good, and he has to learn what is bad. It is the same way for those who come into a relationship with Christ. You have to learn to hear His voice, and you have to learn to feel His presence. You have to learn when to speak, and you have to learn when to listen. You have to learn when to move forward, and you have to learn when to stand still. You learn by reading His word because this is your instruction manual. Everything you need is in the manual, and as you are reading, if you are not quite comprehending, you know you have a relationship with the writer of the manual. When you come to Him and you ask "As I read so and so in your word, I do not quite comprehend". Because of who He is, even though He is so great, He can simplify it so that you can understand what your expectations are.

This is an individual question and it shall get an individual answer from Me (God). What should you be doing as you are waiting? It is a process and you must understand that it involves time, it involves planning, and it involves giving all of yourself unto Him. This whole thing is a very integral part of the process is you giving yourself solely unto Him, and allowing Him to do what He needs to do to break down the purging, the building up, the waiting, the standing still, and the building of relationships of what not to say and when to speak. While I am sitting just waiting on Him in that place does it make that place the right place? It does not necessarily have to be the same place every day because He dwells in the secret place of your heart. Designate in that secret place of your heart saying "Lord I am open to do what needs to be done," and if you do not mean what you are saying, do not speak it, because I will remind you again that the power of life and death is in your tongue. So if you are going to speak life over your situation that means that you totally give yourself to Me (God) to do what needs to be done in that waiting process.

I understand now that it is not about my time but Your divine time to do what you need to do. Because I understand that at the end of this waiting process as I come out as You have promised in Your Word I shall be as pure gold. I shall be shining not only in Your eyes, but to those that are going to be drawn unto me because it is through that refining process that I will be able to tell others this is what happened to me in my season of waiting. Waiting is a season, it is not a time.

How Do You Wait? - A Call To Action

Chapter 10— Notes

Conclusion

God's instructions have been to the people of God to go ye therefore into the world teaching and preaching and to use the gifts that He has given them in order to tell others of the goodness of Jesus Christ. There is no definitive way of how He uses them, and who He chooses to use. It is only a willingness, that they are willing to do no matter what it is they have to go through knowing they will come through victorious.

It is my promise to you that as I open myself up and be transparent to the world, and the world being those who will read the words in this book, and it is so much more than just a book, that it will be a testament to some, an instruction manual for some, a ray of hope to some, and a deliverance to others. As you read and understand that, the same way God has brought me through, God's word to you is that surely if He did it for me, this same God can do it for you.

There is a saying that says "No Pain No Gain." Even though sometimes the pain may have been self-afflicted, if you do not learn through the process there is no gain. My prayer for you as you read this book, is that you will gain without the unnecessary pain because your spiritual eyes will be open, your hearts will be open, and your spirit will be open, and you will be willing to accept what is being said.

I pray that you will take it in, and move forward, and not only will you finish this book, but as God places someone on your heart, you will share it with them. So my prayer is as you are freely delivered by this book that others will be the same. It is a mes-

outside the will of Christ when everything that we have we can gain in our season of waiting. If there is one thing I want you to gain from reading this book is the importance of waiting on Him. So I say to you, wait on the Lord and be of good courage and He shall (for it is His promise) strengthen your heart. Wait, I say, on the Lord (Psalm 27:14)

> *14 Wait on the Lord: be of good courage, and he shall strengthen thine heart: wait, I say, on the Lord.*

CAROLYN J. BLUE is the founder of Embracing It Now, Inc. and The Balanced Room in southeastern North Carolina with over twenty-five years of teaching experience. She is an ordained minister and a certified balance coach.

The Balance Coach is a transformational speaker, a sought out conference speaker, and co-author of *The Teen Handbook of Self Confidence*. She lives in Leland, North Carolina with her husband Eric G. Blue, Sr. and daughter Veronda Turguoise Blue.

While I Wait

www.ingramcontent.com/pod-product-compliance
Lightning Source LLC
Chambersburg PA
CBHW021118080526
44587CB00010B/556